Bill Clinton's Guide to

Appropriate Behavior

Completely Unabridged Version

by

Turner Luce

and

Phyllis Steen

Edited by Joe Kerr

Published by the Humor Department of

Great Little Book Publishing Co., Inc.
Sacramento, CA

Bill Clinton's Guide to Appropriate Behavior –
Unabridged.

Copyright © 2016 by Karl W. Palachuk.

All rights reserved.

Notice: Bill Clinton is not personally involved in this
project. This is an unauthorized summary.

ISBN: 978-1-942115-15-1 (Paperback)
ISBN: 978-1-942115-18-2 (Kindle)

Note:

This is a **blank gift book**, intended to bring joy into
your life. Feel free to fill the inside pages with your own
thoughts and jokes.

If you would like to find more Blank books – or create
your own as a gift – visit **www.BlankGiftBook.com**.

Bill Clinton's Guide to Appropriate Behavior

Notes:

_____

_____

_____

_____

_____

_____

_____

_____

More Titles in This Series . . .
From BlankGiftBook.com

What You Should Expect from Your Ex-Wife
by Mia Culpa

The Big Guide to Honest Politicians
by Pat McCann

How to Make Women Feel Better During Menopause
by Les Moody

How to Be an Attorney and Keep Your Soul
by Sue First

The Complete Guide to Humility for MDs
by Anita Procedure

How to Find Job Security in Corporate America
by Justin Case

What Men Know About Making Women Feel Special
by Mike Easter

. . . And you can even create your own Blank Gift Book at

www.BlankGiftBook.com!